GO DUCK HUNTING!

by
Lisa M. Bolt Simons

CAPSTONE PRESS
a capstone imprint

Captivate is published by Capstone Press, an imprint of Capstone.
1710 Roe Crest Drive, North Mankato, Minnesota 56003
www.capstonepub.com

Library of Congress Cataloging-in-Publication Data
Names: Simons, Lisa M. B., 1969- author.
Title: Go duck hunting! / by Lisa M. Bolt Simons.
Description: North Mankato, Minnesota : Capstone Press, [2022] |
Series: The wild outdoors | Includes bibliographical references and
index. | Audience: Ages 8-11 | Audience: Grades 4-6 | Summary: "A duck
hunter crouches in a camouflage tent called a blind. Suddenly, a flock of
ducks takes flight from the water. The hunter has one chance to take the
shot! Readers will learn about the gear, weapons and skills they need to
enjoy this exciting outdoor sport"— Provided by publisher.
Identifiers: LCCN 2021002785 (print) | LCCN 2021002786 (ebook) |
ISBN 9781663906038 (hardcover) | ISBN 9781663920478 (paperback) |
ISBN 9781663906007 (pdf) | ISBN 9781663906021 (kindle edition)
Subjects: LCSH: Duck shooting—Juvenile literature.
Classification: LCC SK333.D8 S54 2022 (print) | LCC SK333.D8 (ebook) |
DDC 799.2/44—dc23
LC record available at https://lccn.loc.gov/2021002785
LC ebook record available at https://lccn.loc.gov/2021002786

Image Credits
Alamy: David Wei, 29, Jeffery Isaac Greenberg 20+, 21, Steve
Oehlenschlager, 8, 17; Capstone Studio: Karon Dubke, 11, 14; Getty
Images: iStock/saz1977, 1, Mike Kezar, 15, 24; Granger: Sarin Images, 7;
Shutterstock: AnnaForlenza, 16, Brian N Rogers, 5, Creaturart Images,
22, Dennis Jacobsen, Cover, Kirk Geisler, 13, Konjushenko Vladimir, 26,
MaxShutter, 18, rodimov, 12, 19, Steve Oehlenschlager, 20, Victor Tyakht,
23, Vigen M, 25

Editorial Credits
Editor: Mandy Robbins; Designer: Jennifer Bergstrom; Media
Researcher: Jo Miller; Production Specialist: Tori Abraham

Printed in the United States   5426

Table of Contents

Words in **bold** are in the glossary.

ON THE HUNT!

It's early morning. You're sitting in a **duck blind** on the edge of a lake. The shelter means you don't have to sit still or be quiet like you do when you're hunting other animals. You're hidden from the ducks as you wait for them to fly in. You hope they see your **decoys**.

You scouted the area yesterday and saw ducks fly in and out of the lake. You're dressed in **camouflage**. Your gun is ready. Your dog is next to you, ready to **retrieve** your kill. As you wait for the ducks to fly closer, you use your duck call.

You hear them coming and get quiet. Then you see them in the sky. You feel your blood pumping. You raise your gun as they head toward the lake. It's time to take your shot!

A duck hunter waits in a duck blind for ducks to appear.

FACT

Ducks are found on every continent in the world,
except for Antarctica.

Chapter 1

A HISTORY OF WATERFOWL PRESERVATION

Hunting dates back to when humans first roamed the planet. They hunted animals, including waterfowl, for food. Waterfowl are birds that need a water **habitat** to survive. Ducks are part of the waterfowl family. They are found in lakes, rivers, wetlands, and oceans.

In the 1800s and early 1900s, the United States didn't have any laws or rules about hunting waterfowl. In a single day on the East Coast, 15,000 canvasback ducks were shot. If this continued, there would soon be no waterfowl left in the area.

Duck hunters asked for laws to protect waterfowl. Laws helped, but hunters also wanted to protect the places where waterfowl lived. This means keeping their homes safe for the waterfowl. President Theodore Roosevelt started the National Wildlife Refuge System to do this in 1903.

An 1888 engraving of a duck hunter in action

A pair of duck hunters look for a good place to hunt.

Today, duck hunting is popular for many reasons. Unlike with some types of hunting, duck hunters don't have to be quiet. When ducks are flying, hunters can talk to each other. They can also move around more. Only when ducks approach the water is it time to focus and be quiet.

Duck hunters see a lot of action. Because ducks fly, the hunter has to call them to the water. Hunters use duck calls and other gear. After the birds have been shot, they must be retrieved, often by dogs. There are a lot of sightings, shooting opportunities, and activity involved.

There are several kinds of duck **species** to hunt. Seeking out different kinds of ducks makes duck hunting even more of a fun challenge.

FACT

Duck hunters don't have to use scent killers like some other hunters do. One popular scent killer when deer hunting is deer pee!

Chapter 2

GEARING UP

You need some gear before you go duck hunting. A weapon is a must. Most hunters use a shotgun and **ammunition**. Common shotguns are 12 gauges or 20 **gauges**. The gauge is the width inside the gun's barrel. Most shotguns have a 28- to 30-inch (71- to 76-centimeter) long barrel. Some have **sights**, which help aim.

Some hunters prefer a bow. Bows require extra skill. Using a bow usually means choosing a smaller body of water, like a pond or small swamp. Then the hunter will be closer to the target.

Bowhunters have different arrow tips to choose from. JUDO points are arrows often used for small game, such as waterfowl. JUDO points are a type of blunt arrowhead. Blunt arrowheads don't actually cut into their target. It's the impact of the arrow that kills the animal.

Hunting shotguns can have a variety of designs.

A hunter wears special high rubber boots to walk into streams and ponds.

Hunters need more gear than just their weapons. Sometimes just getting to your hunting site requires special gear. Duck hunters sometimes need a boat or a canoe to get to the hunting site. They can even hunt from the boat.

What hunters wear is important, too. Ducks have good eyesight, so camouflage, dark, or black clothing is best. If you don't have a dog to retrieve for you, make sure you wear waders or hip boots. These rubber pieces of clothing keep you dry when you're walking through water.

Duck hunters usually wear duck calls around their necks on a cord or rope. Duck calls come in different colors and styles. Duck hunters learn how to make specific sounds to attract the ducks.

A Duck Hunter's Best Friend

Dogs aren't a must-have for duck hunting. But if you have one, you're part of history. Breeders started developing hunting dogs starting in the 1700s, with more than 50 breeds. Sir Dudley Marjoribanks, who later became Lord Tweedmouth, bred the first golden retrievers in the mid-1800s in Scotland. Hunting dogs popular today include retrievers, spaniels, and pointers.

A chocolate labrador retriever finds a downed duck.

Other gear will help make your duck hunt successful. Hunters often use decoys. These fake ducks are painted to look like ones you're hunting. Hunters place decoys in the water. You can use a few of them in small streams or ponds. You can use more in large lakes. Then real ducks will see the decoys and think it is a safe place to land.

Mallard duck decoys

Hunters shoot from behind a duck blind.

Some hunters use a duck blind. This shelter protects you from the weather. It also keeps you from being seen by ducks. If you choose to use a duck blind, make sure it blends in with your environment. You can also use natural cover, such as prairie grass or cattails.

Chapter 3

RULES AND RESPONSIBILITIES

You must learn the rules of duck hunting before you go. In many places, hunting education courses are required. When you're ready to hunt, remember that each area has its own laws. With a few exceptions, hunters must have a **license**. If you hunt on public land, such as a national

Always get permission before hunting on private property.

wildlife refuge, check the rules. If you want to hunt on private property, make sure it's okay with the owner.

There are plenty of rules to keep in mind. Use a shotgun that does not hold more than three shells. Do not hunt from a motor vehicle, such as an all-terrain vehicle (ATV). Only hunt during daylight hours and during the hunting season. Pay attention to the daily duck limit. For example, you may only be able to bring home five ducks a day.

A young hunter poses with his kill.

FACT

Money paid to buy licenses, fees, special duck stamps, gear, and ammunition help buy land for wildlife. This effort helps **conserve** land for wildlife and future hunting opportunities.

A man doing target practice

Before you go hunting, make sure you practice shooting. You can practice hitting sporting clays at a skeet or trap course. Skeet and trap courses are fields that have shooting stations and trap houses. A machine in the trap house randomly launches the clay targets for shooters to try to hit.

Practicing shooting this way helps you practice hitting a target at different times and angles. Since ducks fly from all over, hitting clay targets flying in different directions is good practice.

The goal is to kill a duck as quickly as possible, hopefully with the first shot. Once you hit a duck, make sure it's dead. If it's still moving, you may need to shoot it again before it dives underwater.

A hunter takes aim at a duck.

A hunting dog retrieves the kill.

An important part of duck hunting is retrieving the bird. Even if it's wounded, hunters must make every effort to find a downed duck.

Some hunters own dogs that do the job for them. Dogs have an amazing sense of smell. They can find the spot where a duck went down. But the duck hunter must be willing to put in time to train the dog. A dog with a good bond to the hunter combined with good training should make a great retriever.

Other hunters don't own dogs. It is still their responsibility to find the ducks they shoot. Having waders or hip boots might be necessary. Sometimes having a canoe or small boat can be helpful.

The Duck Stamp Act

In the early 1900s, waterfowl numbers were dropping fast. Restaurants had birds on menus. People used feathers for clothes and hats. In 1934, President Franklin D. Roosevelt signed the Duck Stamp Act. According to this act, special duck stamps would be sold to raise money to protect waterfowl habitats. Duck hunters must purchase one. Today, a yearly art contest determines what the stamp will look like. At least 1.5 million stamps are sold every year.

National Wildlife Refuge sign

Chapter 4

INS AND OUTS OF DUCK HUNTING

There are four main groups of ducks found in North America: puddle ducks, diving ducks, sea ducks, and whistling ducks.

Mallard ducks take flight.

The mallard duck is probably the most recognized and well known. Three others are popular to hunt: the green-winged teal, the northern pintail, and the American wigeon. All of these ducks are puddle ducks. Wood ducks, black ducks, and mottled ducks are also puddle ducks.

Common diving ducks include redheads, canvasbacks, buffleheads, and goldeneyes. Longtails are sea ducks. Black-bellied whistling ducks are, well, whistling ducks.

Common goldeneye ducks float peacefully.

Other kinds of ducks can be found all over the world. In Asia, there are almost 40 species of ducks to hunt. And in Australia, hunters target the Pacific black duck, the Australian wood duck, teal ducks, the pink-eared duck, and the mountain duck.

FACT

The biggest duck in North America weighs 6 pounds (3 kilograms). It is the common eider.

Two hunters wait for ducks to fly overhead.

When it comes to duck hunting, safety comes first. Young hunters need adult supervision. Young hunters can learn a lot from the experiences of older hunters. In some places, it's about helping a young hunter stay safe. In many, it's the law.

Young hunters take gun safety courses before hunting. They will learn safety rules to remember while handling a firearm. **Muzzle** control is when the shotgun is pointed in a safe direction. A shotgun's safety should be on until it's ready to be fired. This part of the gun keeps it from firing. The hunter's finger should stay outside of the trigger guard. Only move the finger inside the guard when it's time to shoot.

A short-barreled hunting shotgun

A hunter takes a shot from his raft.

Whether a hunter uses a shotgun or a bow, they must follow many safety rules. First, a hunter needs to know where the other hunters are located. Make sure you look around and know where they are. It is especially important to do this when duck hunting clothing is camouflage or dark. Duck hunters should keep personal space in order to shoot safely. They should also have a shooting lane. A shooting lane is a pathway to the target. Try not to shoot in another hunter's shooting lane.

Hunters should not retrieve any ducks until all hunters have shot their guns or bows. If hunters have shotguns, they can open the **action** or put the guns on their shoulder. Then they retrieve the ducks.

There are lots of places to duck hunt. Each one will have its own rules, season, and hours to hunt. Each location also offers a different duck species to hunt.

You can hunt in almost all 50 United States. Duck hunting is also allowed in Mexico and Canada. Many other countries around the world allow duck hunting. They include Argentina, Mongolia, Azerbaijan, and Pakistan.

Duck hunters can find different areas to hunt. There are wildlife management areas. There are public lands. You may even know someone with private land who would allow you to hunt there.

Duck hunting is an activity that allows you to hunt in a variety of waterways. It takes practice, ability, and responsibility. With time, you may become a duck hunter for life!

A duck hunter poses with his kills.

GLOSSARY

action (AK-shuhn)—the part of the gun that loads, fires, and ejects the ammunition cartridge

ammunition (am-yuh-NI-shuhn)—bullets and other objects that can be fired from weapons

camouflage (KAM-uh-flahzh)—coloring or covering that makes animals, people, and objects blend in

conserve (kuhn-SURV)—to keep safe and not destroy

decoy (DEE-koi)—a fake animal used in hunting

duck blind (DUHK BLYND)—a shelter used for hunting

gauge (GAYJ)—the size of the inside of a gun barrel

habitat (HAB-uh-tat)—the natural place and conditions in which a plant or animal lives

license (LYE-suhnss)—a document showing permission to do something

muzzle (MUHZ-uhl)—the mouth or end of a gun

retrieve (rih-TREEV)—to bring back

sight (SITE)—a piece of equipment used on a weapon to help a hunter aim

species (SPEE-sheez)—a group of animals with similar features

READ MORE

Carpenter, Tom. *Duck Hunting.* Lake Elmo, MN: Focus Readers, 2018.

Doeden, Matt. *Duck Hunting.* Mankato, MN: Amicus High Interest, Amicus Ink, 2017.

Garstecki, Julia. *Birding.* North Mankato, MN: Capstone Press, 2022.

INTERNET SITES

Duck Wing Identification
fws.gov/hunting/wing-id.html

Junior Duck Stamp Conservation Program
fws.gov/birds/education/junior-duck-stamp-conservation-program.php

Waterfowl ID
ducks.org/hunting/waterfowl-id/

INDEX